EVERYTHING YOU NEED TO KNOW ABOUT

NEGOTIATION SKILLS

A Concise and Comprehensive Guide for Everyone

B. HUGHES MSC MCIPS

Copyright © 2013 Billy Hughes
All rights reserved.
ISBN: 1483941205
ISBN 13: 9781483941202

CONTENTS

- **1**   INTRODUCTION
- **3**   NEGOTIATION – WHAT IS IT
- **5**   NEGOTIATION PROCESS –THE 3 PHASES
- **7**   NEGOTIATION PHASE I - PREPARATION
  - Goals & Objectives
  - Aspiration Levels
  - Strategy
  - BATNAS
  - Agenda
  - Information
- **15**   NEGOTIATION PHASE I I - IN PROCESS
  - Harmonics
  - ZOPAS
  - Tactics
- **19**   NEGOTIATION PHASE III - CLOSING THE DEAL
  - Delay
  - MOU
  - Batna
- **23**   STRATEGY REVISITED
  - Integrative Strategy
  - Distributive Strategy
  - Positional Strategy
  - Principled Strategy
  - Positional v Principled
- **29**   TACTICS REVISITED – TACTICS THAT WORK
- **35**   CONCESSION PATTERNS
- **37**   POWER – SOURCES OF POWER
- **41**   PNP – PERSONAL NEGOTIATING POWER
- **43**   PSYCHOLOGY IN NEGOTIATION
- **45**   LAW OF BUSINESS BALANCE
- **47**   DO'S IN NEGOTIATION
- **49**   DON'TS IN NEGOTIATION

1

INTRODUCTION

**Billy Hughes
MSc MCIPS**

Hi, I'm Billy Hughes. I've been operating in the global business world for over twenty-five years, fifteen of those in senior Purchasing and Procurement Management positions, and a further ten in leadership roles in Sales & Marketing with a number of world class companies.

I've also been and in and through the education system for much if not most of my life, from primary - kindergarten to some, through to successfully gaining a Postgrad Master's Degree to complement a proudly held Purchasing Degree. I believe that this gives me a unique insight into one of the most important and valuable areas of expertise required in both business and personal life and which is usually only taught in specialist courses, generally out with school and college curriculum.

It doesn't matter whether you are self-employed, or whether you are a Scientist, Financier, Engineer, Teacher or if you work internal to an organisation, or both internal and external. It makes no difference whether you are a student, a politician or that you work for a non-profit organisation.

One of the single biggest skills you must have, without question, is – the Ability to Negotiate, effectively.

In the cost conscious high speed world economy those who negotiate for their companies, and this includes many whose functions are out with Procurement and Sales, are under enormous pressure from their internal and external customers to deliver beneficial outcomes regarding cost, cost containment, cost reduction and value.

To not only sustain competitiveness, but to survive.

In your personal life at some point you will have to make major investments, - buying a house, a car, holidays. At work you will change jobs which will have salary and terms implications, and every day you will have to deal with your loved ones and those not so loved. You are negotiating everyday of your lives; it will benefit you to learn how to do it well. This Guide will be a massive help to your understanding of the Negotiation Process and provide tools and techniques to improve your ability to do better, more often, guaranteed.

It isn't a spectator sport and you will be involved anyway so use what you learn.

2

NEGOTIATION – WHAT IS IT?

❝..a process involving dealing among people intended to result in an agreement and commitment to a course of action… ❞

❝….The use of information and power to affect behaviour within a web of tension ❞ Herb Cohen – You Can Negotiate Anything 1980

So what we are looking for is to make a deal of some kind. Cohen talks about a " web of tension " and this is very appropriate because very many negotiations involve intense emotional pressure at some point. It is easy to talk Win-Win, much more difficult to achieve.

3

NEGOTIATION PROCESS – 3 PHASES

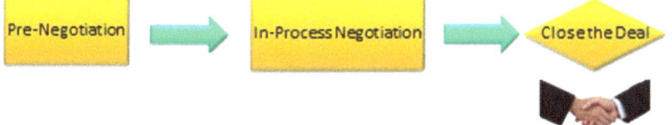

This is a simplified model of the actual negotiation cycle from beginning to end. The reality is more complex. We'll start with the Pre-Negotiation phase.

4

PHASE I PRE-NEGOTIATION PROCESS - PREPARATION

P reparation in negotiation is vital. Abraham Lincoln stated that if he had eight hours to cut down a tree he'd spend six hours sharpening the axe. We won't always have eight minutes never mind eight hours but having an in-depth knowledge of negotiation coupled with speed of thought will more often than not get us a better outcome.

We'll have a review of some of the key factors to address regarding the preparation required starting with the goals and objectives.

Negotiation Process Flow

Goals & Objectives

The necessity of setting the Goals and Objectives cannot be underestimated. The advantages of setting the goals and documenting them are two-fold, one to help you prepare properly but also remembering that the Negotiations themselves can be intensely

emotional – it helps you to refer back and perhaps also to step back, in the heat of the Negotiation moment. Experts have also realised that there appears to be an inherent power through documenting your goals.

It is also worth pointing out at this stage that it is valuable to also consider the outcomes the other person/organisation wishes to have. Ultimately for a successful negotiation both sides important needs will have to be met to a greater or lesser degree.

Regarding Tools for the Goal Setting process I find the Kepner Tregoe models good whereby you set your Musts, Wants and Needs. This helps to bring some formality and rationale to the process. Everyone on the team, or in the background to the team, will have an opinion as to what is important. This helps to formalise the thought framework. It can also help to identify some 'straw issues' which can be used as part of your concession strategy, which we will discuss later.

Aspiration Levels

When setting your goals and objectives aim high, studies have shown that the higher you aim the more successful you are likely to be - aim for the stars and you may well land on the moon.

*I worked for a menial's hire,
Only to learn dismayed,
That any wage I asked of life
Life would have paid*

J.B. Rittenhouse

Strategy

" Victory in battle is apparent to all, but the science of ensuring victory before the battle begins is a skill known but to a few " Sun Tzu Ancient China 475 B.C.

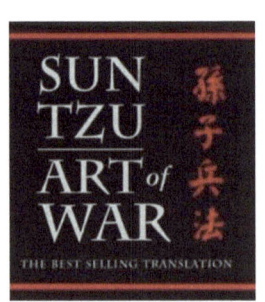

There is a multitude of labels now in use for different Negotiation Strategies that can be adopted. However the important thing to remember is that they all relate in some way and to varying degrees to either a Lose-Lose, Win - Lose or Win -Win situation for all involved parties. Since Karass's time the names put forward include Integrative, Principled, Distributive and Positional – none of them mutually exclusive as win-win is in the eye of the beholder and even if the pie gets bigger it still has to be distributed, i.e.

shared. **These are discussed and explained in more depth in later chapters.**

Negotiation Strategies

Win-Win — Win

Partnership
Collaborative
Principled
Integrative

Adversarial
Competitive
Distributive

Positional

Lose — Lose-Lose

PBS

BATNAS

BATNA's are your Best Alternative to a Negotiated Agreement, the term coined by Ury & Fisher in Getting to Yes.

For example if you are looking to buy a house, a better alternative to getting locked in to a purchase of more than you can afford may be to look at renting for a period till the market goes down. Instead of buying the car you thought you would get for a knockdown price you decide that yes you can keep your old rust-bucket for another year, the repairs cost may be a better solution at this time. BATNAS are a very useful concept for a number of other reasons.

Take the extreme of an Auction. In the heat of the moment you can get emotionally carried away, feel the need to 'win' at all costs during the auction process itself, and ultimately getting an extremely bad deal for yourself and your wallet.

Having established a walkaway point and generated alternatives beforehand you are less likely to do so. BATNAS can also help you to understand that your walkaway point is perhaps lower than it should be – cutting off your nose to spite your face. A major benefit is that it can also toughen your resolve in the heat of the negotiation process itself when you are coming under pressure to concede.

Agendas

Agendas are actually a very powerful tool, much underestimated in business but not in Politics.

The key message is to Learn from the Politicians. Some of the reasons why Agendas are powerful:
- Can help predetermine the outcomes through proper planning
- The person who controls the Agenda controls the agenda items i.e.
- what is on the agenda and sometimes more importantly what is not.

PHASE I PRE- NEGOTIATION PROCESS - PREPARATION

Time	Duration	Subject: Very interesting. Venue Room 666. Date: 18-09-2020	Owner
08.30	0.30	Welcome	You
09.00	0.30	New Products Overview	Tech Manager
09.30	0.30	Customer Strategy	Sales Manager
10.00	0.30	Break	All
10.30	1 Hour	Working Session	All
11.30	1 Hour	Break-out Session	All
12.30	0.30	Lunch	All

- The person who controls the agenda can define who and does not attend the meetings
- The agenda represents an opportunity to gain and hold the initiative.
- Those who control the agenda can formulate the questions and time the decisions.
- A good agenda can clarify or hide motives.

Information

" if you truly know the enemy and yourself you need not fear the result of one hundred battles, if you know yourself but not the enemy, for every victory gained you will also suffer a defeat. If you know neither the enemy nor yourself you will succumb in every battle. " Sun Tzu – Ancient China 475 B.C.

Knowledge with use is power, accrue as much information as you possibly can to support the negotiation.

Sources of Information
- Suppliers
- Marketplace
- Competition
- Internet
- Professional Bodies
- Others

Important sources to bolster your information include all of these.

To repeat knowledge with use is power - remember Sun Tzu.

5

PHASE II - IN-PROCESS NEGOTIATION

With all this preparation we've put ourselves in an excellent position to have a positive outcome from stage two of the process, the negotiation itself.

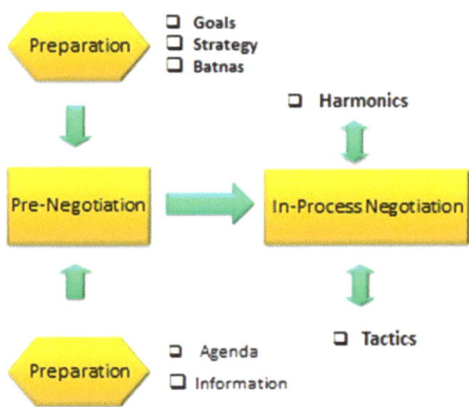

Negotiation Process Flow

Remember the underlying reason behind a negotiation " a process involving dealing among people which are intended to resulting an agreement and commitment to a course of action… "Through the goal setting process you have set your realistically high target price, your walk away price, and a price you can live with. The party you're dealing with may or may not have gone through this formal process, but will have an idea or feeling for this.

Harmonics - The Negotiation Dance – Offer & Counter Offer

What tends to happen in the majority of Positional or Distributive Negotiations is that most parties will have a target range, developed formally, informally or intuitively. You may have set out with your realistically high opening offer. The other party, may Flinch (see Tactics), and make you a counter offer, realistically low, you Flinch, and so the dance begins. This is called Negotiation Harmonics.

ZOPA – Zone of Possible Agreement

If both parties are serious then what tends to happen is that there is a ZOPA– a range or Zone of Possible Agreement as seen in the diagram. The most skilled negotiator will come out on top within the ZOPA range.

PHASE II - IN-PROCESS NEGOTIATION

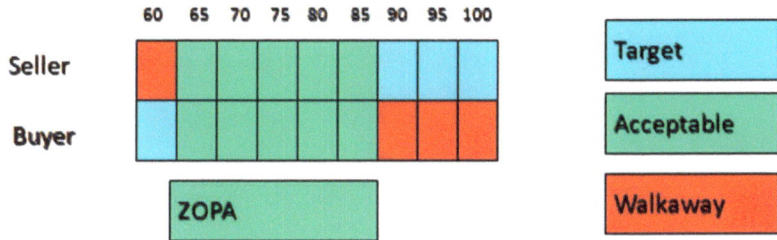

Tactics

We spoke earlier about Strategy which is the Master Plan.

Tactics is " the science off organising and manoeuvring forces in battle; the individual steps to support a strategy carried out concurrently or in parallel ." Tactics are in large part situational. The key words above include " to support a strategy" so

the tactics you utilise will in large part be dependent on the strategy you have adopted. However the strategy that you have adopted may not be the strategy of the people across the table so you also have to be very aware of tactics that are being used against you. " If you truly know the enemy and yourself you need not fear the result of one hundred battles, *if you know yourself but not the enemy, for every victory gained you will also suffer a defeat. If you know neither the enemy nor yourself you will succumb in every battle."* Sun Tzu – Ancient China 475 B.C.

We've set up to show a two way arrow for tactics in the Negotiation Cycle presentation. This is to highlight that during the process itself you have to flexible. If something isn't working you may want or need to be able to change. There is no "One Best Way". Focus on the outcome and on whatever it takes to get there.

We'll go on to discuss some that work and some that have been almost certainly been used against you in Tactics Revisited.

6

PHASE III – CLOSING THE DEAL

So in a simplified 3 stage model we are getting toward the close. However a word of caution – negotiations rarely go so smoothly. I've input the delay icon for two reasons. One it can be a deliberate tactic by either side to put pressure into the system, or it could be that one or both parties may have to go back to their relevant 'camps' and get internal agreement.

Negotiation Process Flow

BATNA

However, despite everyone's best efforts even within a collaborative, co-operatively spirited negotiation it may just be the case that your BATNA– best alternative to a negotiated agreement, is your better option, in this case you or the other party walk away. No deal is better than a bad deal.

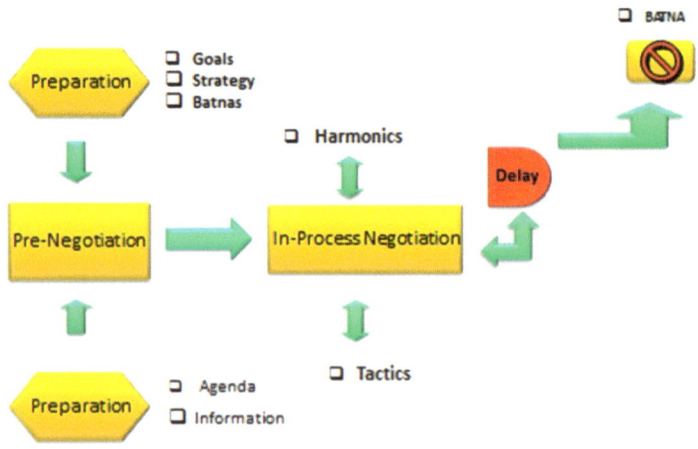

MOU – Memorandum of Understanding

However, after all the sweat and hard work, you've struck a good deal. An actual contract can in some cases take months and years to nail down between parties. An interim solution to get things moving is to draw up a short form contract or MOU. The Wise Negotiator will document this. Some people can be just plain lazy and this can be to your advantage even at this late stage, making sure that at least your important points are nailed down.

MOU – Memorandum of Understanding (cont) example – use your own

MOU Template
(Essential Elements)

I. **Parties to the MOU**
- The MOU should identify the name and address (principal place of business) of the partner(s) as well as the Federal, State or local programs that they are representing in this agreement.

II. **Duration of Agreement**
- This is a statutorily required element. While the length of the initial agreement is negotiable between the local board and the partner(s), all MOUs should initially be for a period of at least one year. Modification, extension, and termination procedures are described in a separate section of this template document.

III. **One-Stop System Overview**
- This section of the MOU should briefly describe the Local Workforce Investment Board's vision of the One-Stop system, its partnerships and comprehensive One-Stop center(s), affiliates and satellite sites. Discuss the "as is" as well as the "to be" plans (strategic vision) for the local system.

- Any mission statement, general purpose statement and/or operating principles that partners have collectively agreed to pursue on behalf of the local workforce investment system should be included in this section as appropriate.

- A map (or diagram) with the centers/affiliates/electronic access points identified and a written listing of sites by address with program operator(s) identified should also be included as an attachment to the MOU.

- Identify how the One-Stop system will ensure compliance with the Americans with Disabilities Act to ensure accessibility to customers with disabilities and other pertinent special populations within the local area. Describe how discrimination complaints will be handled and how reasonable accommodation costs will be shared.

IV. **One-Stop Performance Requirements and Goals**
- Reporting Assurances - The following assurances should be included in each MOU:
    1. All partners in the One-Stop Delivery system will adhere to any prescribed reporting schedules.
    2. All partners in the One-Stop Delivery system will provide any required performance data.
    3. All partners in the One-Stop Delivery system will provide any required data in a compatible format.
    4. All partners in the One-Stop Delivery system agree to work toward the development of common performance goals and measures that will be in alignment with the stated goals of the workforce investment system.

7

STRATEGY REVISITED

Strategy – What it Is

…..the science or art of planning and conducting a war or military campaign– no different really from many aspects of business." Victory in battle is apparent to all, but the science of ensuring victory before the battle begins is a skill known but to a few "Sun Tzu Ancient China 475 B.C. Sun Tzu was a general but he was also a priest, philosopher and pacifist. He was a master at understanding conflict but also knew how to hasten peace.

We can differentiate this from Tactics which is The science of organising and manoeuvring forces in battle; the individual steps to support a strategy carried out sequentially, concurrently or in parallel.

Strategy Revisited - Different Types
Integrative Strategy – Win/Win

Often spoke about, difficult to achieve, but nevertheless worth the effort in the long term. This is a Collaborative strategy in which parties attempt to find a Win-Win solution. Focuses on developing mutually beneficial agreements based on the needs, desires, concerns and fears important to each side - attempts to enlarge the pie, but again this needs to be sliced.

Distributive Strategy - Win / Lose
Based on the principle of competition between participants. Usually ends up win-lose to some degree.

Positional Strategy - Lose Lose - Win / Lose
This involves holding onto a fixed idea or position of what you want and arguing for it and it alone regardless of underlying interests. Tends to be the first strategy people adopt when entering a negotiation.
Positional negotiation is less likely to result in a win-win outcome due to entrenchment and the adversarial behaviour can cause long term ill feeling.

However compromise may be better than no agreement.

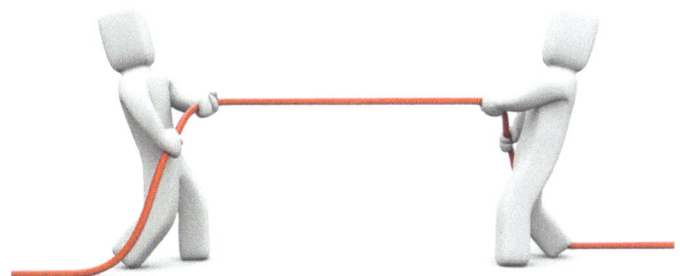

Principled Strategy - Again looking to Win-Win
This is the name given to the interest-based approach to negotiation set out in Getting To Yes – Ury & Fisher 1981.

The approach advocates four fundamental principles of negotiation:-
- Separate the People from the Problem
- Focus on Interests and not Positions
- Invent Options for Mutual Gain
- Insist on Objective Criteria

Separating the people from the problem as a concept is extremely inviting as negotiations involve people who have their own agendas, opinions and motivations.

Focusing on interests and not Positions – this is easier said than done as most people's first strategy is to dig themselves into a Position and then justify it.

Inventing the Options for Mutual gain is trying to increase the pie for both parties.

Insisting on Objective Criteria is a useful strategy as emotions during the process can run high. Good examples of objective criteria include:-
- The law uses Precedent
- Finance can use industry standard Indices e.g. FT for exchange rates.

Some critics of Principled Negotiation feel that the use & abuse of POWER is underestimated for and in this style of Negotiation, however it is a logical and intuitively sound framework from which to build upon. Power and people's emotions will be hurdles to overcome.

Positional v Principled Strategy – A Comparison
This comparison allows us a fairly black and white view of the spectrum of available negotiation strategies. I would repeat that none are mutually exclusive but to be aware **of them is to have power.**

STRATEGY REVISITED

Positional v Principled

Positional	Principled
Adversaries	Joint Problem Solvers
Goal is Victory	Goal is Wise Decision
Demand Concessions	Work Together
Dig into Position	Focus on Interests
Use Tricks, mislead	Open & Fair
Insist on Position	Objective Criteria
Apply pressure	Yield to principle
Win for you alone outlook	Look for win-win

8

TACTICS REVISITED – TACTICS THAT WORK

We spoke earlier about Strategy which is the Master Plan. To repeat, tactics is**" the science of organising and manoeuvring forces in battle; the individual steps to support a strategy carried out sequentially, concurrently or in parallel** "Tactics are in large part situational. The key words above include " to support a strategy" so the tactics you utilise will in large part be dependent on the strategy you have adopted. There is no "One Best Way". Focus on the outcome and on whatever it takes to get there…...and do remember that the strategy that you have adopted may not be the strategy of the people across the table so you also have to be very aware of tactics that are being used against you – remember Sun Tzu.

" If you truly know the enemy and yourself you need not fear the result ozone hundred battles, if you know yourself but not the enemy, for every victory gained you will also suffer a defeat. If you know neither the enemy nor yourself you will succumb in every battle We'll now go on to discuss some that work and have most certainly been used against you.

8. Tactics That Work – Some Examples

We'll now discuss some of those tactics, and also determine when they are appropriate or inappropriate.
- Test the Water
- The John McEnroe – You cannot be serious
- Aim realistically high and dig in
- Concessions – See separate page on Concession Patterns
- Deadlines
- Acceptance time
- Pareto & Bundling
- Deliberate deadlock
- The Crunch
- Higher Authority

Testing the Water

Supposing, as in very many cases, we start off in a Positional Negotiation process. Who should make the first offer, and what should it look like. Well if you have a choice it is usually prudent to let the other party give you his opening offer. You may actually be pleasantly surprised. If you have to open, and have done your homework start realistically low. If you haven't done your homework start low anyway. In negotiation what goes up rarely fever comes back down. If they don't take you seriously you can always increase the offer. Studies have shown that more skilful negotiators do this and by doing so fair better more often. For one it gives you room to manoeuvre and two it sets an Aspiration level for the other party.

The John McEnroe

The other party open up with a price. Dramatically you act surprised and say " You cannot be serious........."

Can be combined with **The Squeeze – You've got to do better than that.** This has the impact of lowering the other parties Aspiration Level and also at a later part of the process if and when a deal is struck, psychologically let's him feel good about himself. If you had said oh yes that's sounds like a good price, he/she/they will feel they should have made a lower opening offer and will also start 'nibbling'. However it isn't always possible that the other party can or will make the opening offer – if you have to make the opening offer, what should you do.

Deadlines

Deadlines have amazing power. Watch Estate Agents utilise a closing date. It forces the decision making process and also tends to push prices up. Salesman use the technique all the time – "… prices go up next week…..it is a great bargain at this time…. "Unskilled

negotiators start to give the store away with heavy concession patterns as they fear an agreement won't be reached. What do you do about deadlines. Well the world keeps turning around the sun the next day. Wherever possible move the deadline i.e. you don't always have to accept other people's deadlines.

Pareto & Bundling, Hook & Pull Through

In almost any negotiation there are some very key points important to you. Identify some straw issues and add them to your wish list and make the other party think they are substantial for you. This lets you more easily disguise your overall true needs and allows you to make concessions which are maybe not that significant for you but psychologically the other party may feel that you are showing a willingness to reach compromise. Hey, I'm trying to help the process here. I did this for you – what can you do or me. The other thing that can happen is that if you get agreement on one issue you can perhaps pull another through with it. Someone may just be feeling generous that day or want the negotiation over and done with.

Acceptance Time

Negotiations can get very emotional.

If you've made an offer that you don't want to back away from but the other party is getting angry – at least you know you're getting to their bottom line – then leave it with them to get back to you. People will sometimes rationalise once they are out of the heat of the moment. A friend of mine got to a deadlock situation with a car salesman. He informed the salesman that his final offer was his best can do and to give him a call if he changed his mind. He got a call later that evening.

Deadlock

Deadlock can be a very disturbing psychological situation for people. However don't be afraid to deadlock. Some people use deliberate deadlock very successfully. To show the internal organisation that you are a tough negotiator. To show the other party that you have reached the bottom line. Deadlock is different from an impasse which Dawson in his book on Power Negotiations recommends using a "set-aside" technique to keep the negotiations moving along. **Deadlock itself needs Arbitration or Mediation to break the deadlock.**

Higher Authority

Always have a Higher Authority up your sleeve.
- I need to discuss that with my wife/husband/partner.
- I'll need to take that back to my Organisation.
- I'll need to take that back to my Steering Committee.

This allows you breathing space and thinking time but also to put pressure on the seller. The seller asks you whether you are a decision maker or not. You say only for good decisions.

The Crunch

Have all the sellers/buyers in the waiting room and take one at a time into your office to make their final offer. Not a pleasant way of doing business. Remember, when using tactics remember that they are situational and to be like a Martial Arts Master. Strength is weakness and weakness is strength. There are many more tactics that can be used, I would recommend C.L. Karrass' Give and Take as a starting point.

9

CONCESSION PATTERNS THE TRAPPER STORY.

When you are thinking about making a concession remember the story about the trapper working on his own in the frozen lands of Northern Canada. He's going along the ice plain on his sled pulled by his team of dogs. Out of nowhere come the Wolves, baying and howling. He thinks……. I need to get rid of them – throws them a leg of reindeer from his sled. That'll get rid of them. Yep, he's right, he's on his merry way, happily lonely once again. 20 minutes later, Awoo –oo-oo. Another leg of reindeer. Another 20 minutes, Awoo –oo-oo. By nightfall he's no reindeer left – guess who the wolves are coming after now.

All he did was to encourage them. We're not going to do that.

Concessions - Remember the Wolves

Studies have shown a number of interesting points regarding concession patterns.

Research has found the following:-
- Large initial demands improve the probability of success – gives room for manoeuvre
- Losers tend to make the first concessions
- Losers make the largest concessions in a negotiation
- People who make small concessions fail less
- Skilled negotiators make lower concessions as the Deadline approaches

Recommendations to follow are:-
- Let the other side make theirs first
- Make yours slow and low
- Not quid pro quo
- Lower aspiration levels
- Give away things that don't cost

10

POWER IN NEGOTIATION – SOURCES OF POWER

In a perfect world perhaps share and share alike would be the norm. However any presentation or education on the subject of Negotiation would be absurd without a discussion of Power. Power is of course extremely important in Negotiation and Dawson for example, devotes much of his working life to the topic. There are many Sources of Power which one may not necessarily be conscious of and which can be developed to support the Negotiation Process. Principled Negotiation for example lies fundamentally in the power of fairness – however as we know although we may all be born equal some are born more equal than others – life can be unfair. So we have to develop our power and these are some of the sources we can tap into or actually come up against.

Situational Power
Sometimes this can be unfortunate for you. Have you ever seen anybody get little bit power crazy, where common sense disappears because someone finds themselves in a situation where all of a sudden they have some power over you.

For those who fly have you ever been running late for your flight and the plane is at the gate and they won't let you on. The plane is still sitting there an hour later, drive you nuts.

Expert Power
Technical experts for example are often brought into commercial negotiations to provide a body of knowledge. Their input often goes unchallenged. Can also be the case in the law courts.

Reverent Power
Dawson talks about JF Kennedy & Regan having reverent power, believable and consistent in their behaviour. Mother Theresa could be a very difficult person but she again had reverent power. Gandhi had no formal authority but wielded immense power.

Charismatic Power

It's been said Bill Clinton has this, perhaps doesn't have the Reverent Power though. Princess Diana when she was alive was deemed to have this in spades.

Legitimacy

Legitimate power – the right to succession. Proof, birth certificates, passports, legal documents, titles and so on.

Reward Power

Your boss is an example. Parents. Teachers. They can give and take away.

Precedent

Laws of the land have been heavily influenced by Precedent. The argument to this is that 'times have changed'.

Force

Choose your own example. There are very many sources of power, the important thing to remember is that You have More Power Than You Think – aim high.

11

PNP – PERSONAL NEGOTIATING POWER

As we've said often, negotiations involve people and can be intensely emotional and tiring. Our own Personal Negotiation Power is not static. It fluctuates over time with our Knowledge, Skill and Fitness. To be a great negotiator you'll need all three, and remember you're a human being. Some discerning negotiators will weigh you down with hospitality and kindness.

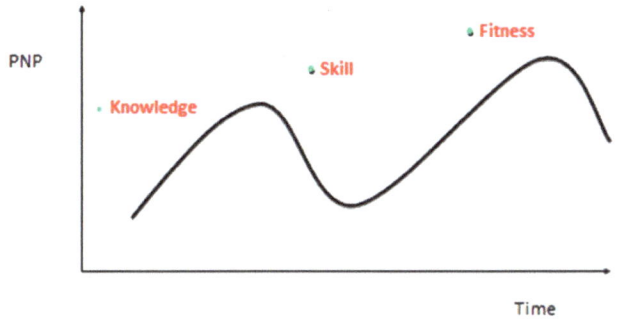

12

NEGOTIATION PSYCHOLOGY

In most Negotiation interaction there are different motivational factors lurking and operating in the background . People have different needs, desires, and aspiration levels and so on and these will have an impact on the vast majority of negotiations. Maslow's Hierarchy Theory is often used to highlight aspects of Motivation. Taken simply if we look at an Organisational Buyer,  his minimum Goals and Objectives may encompass just keeping his job for either security or belonging needs. Therefore he may be unwilling to put himself into a deadlock situation which may challenge his ability to strike a deal. Alternatively, he wants to move up the organisation, wants to show his boss how tough he is, how good a negotiator he is – he may push much harder than most. What may be driving him is belonging, self-esteem or even self-actualisation. At a whole other level someone may just want to strike a deal so he can eat and keep a roof over his head. The wise negotiator will be aware of and try to find out more about the motivational factors that are driving people behind the scenes. Allowing people to 'Grandstand' may be a useful tactic as long as it doesn't get in the way of the eventual targeted Outcomes. Allowing people to 'save face' may go a long way. Dawson, in his Power Negotiations stipulates that you must always make the other party feel good after the negotiation – allow them to believe they have won to some degree and were tough SOB negotiators. Allow people to have won. It may cost you nothing and if you don't it will eventually cost you something.

13

LAW OF BUSINESS BALANCE

Be the best negotiator you possibly can be, work hard to get your just rewards but please remember the very wise words of the 19th Century John Ruskin.

" It is unwise to pay too much but also unwise to pay too little. When you pay too much all you lose is a little money.

But when you pay too little you stand a chance of losing everything because the thing you bought is incapable of doing what you bought it to do.

This common law of business balance prohibits paying a little and getting a lot. It just can't be done. So when you deal with the low bidder it is wise to put a little something aside to take care of the risk you run.

If you can do that, you can afford something better"

John Ruskin – Philosopher

And finally, Negotiation is not a cerebral non-contact sport, you will be involved. Spectating for you will not be an option, you will be in the arena whether you like it or not so give it your best shot and remember that in your lifetime……………..

You won't see too many statues raised to a critic.

14

DO'S LIST

- Do Understand the Negotiation Cycle – Use the Negotiation eCourse
- Do Prepare
- Do Aim High
- Do Write Down Your Goals & Objectives
- Do have the 'team' roles laid out
- Do set your BATNA
- Do Remember that Knowledge with Use is Power
- Do try for a Win-Win, to increase the Pie
- Do remember a Win is in the eye of the beholder
- Do remember the other parties major interest outcomes
- Do Set or influence the Agenda – Learn from the Politicians
- Do have a good variety of Tactics available to you
- Do remember to be Flexible – no one best way
- Do recognise you have 'More Power than you think'
- Do remember Concession patterns – low and slow.
- Do remember the ZOPA's – better negotiators come out better
- Do remember PNP – Personal Negotiating Power
- Do remember Maslow
- Do Practice – not a spectator sport - you are involved anyway
- Do Remember the Law of Business Balance
- Do Remember to congratulate the other parties negotiation ability

15

DON'TS LIST

- Don't be Afraid to Win – be excited
- Don't forget the other Parties interests
- Don't be Inflexible in your thinking – no one best way
- Don't be afraid to walkaway
- Don't Concede like an amateur
- Don't give away your deadline
- Don't fall for tactics that you can nullify
- Don't make quick decisions needlessly
- Don't underestimate your Power
- Don't forget the Law of Business Balance

AUTHOR PROFILE

**Billy Hughes
MSc MCIPS
Billy Hughes
-Bio-**

The author has a rare blend of both Sales and Supply Chain Management leadership experience spanning over twenty years, working with and for world-class companies in the fiercely competitive and fast moving electronics industry covering different market sectors to include Industrial, Government, Telecoms, Computing, Automotive, Medical and Consumer. His working knowledge is global and includes experience at the sharp end in the rapidly expanding Eastern European Countries as well as Central Europe, Western Europe, the Americas, S.E. Asia, India and of course China. He has combined an exceptional vocational background with excellent business and educational qualifications to include an MSc in Materials Management and professional Purchasing Degree. His business philosophy and approach is one of a Practical Partnership.

Life Skills for Business..........Business Skills for Life

www.ingramcontent.com/pod-product-compliance
Lightning Source LLC
Chambersburg PA
CBHW040859180526
45159CB00001B/465